…And I'm Still Standing

Rev. Willie Shell Sr.

DEDICATION

I would like to dedicate this book to my mother Alice Shell, my father Ofield Shell, my wife Elizabeth Shell, my brother Roosevelt Shell, my sister Mary S/Griffin all of whom have gone home to be with the Lord. Their influence in my life made me the person I am today. I would like to thank God for such strong parents, especially my mother.

My brother Kevin Shell Born October 2, 1961, passing on January 4, 1994

My brother Alfonza Shell Born June 6, 1956, passing February 12, 1956

Also my brothers and sisters Andrew, Arbra, Nathaniel, Johnnie, Belinda, Winston

And to a host of many friends who have helped me spiritually and financially

The late Jim Hyson, my sister in law Jeridean.

Good friend Mr. Derrick Steven,

Dr. Harold White, Mr. Donald Good and wife Jennie, Mr. Cobbie Burns,

Attorney Bill Hayn, Attorney Caleb Nichols, Attorney Beverly Fraser, Attorney Jerry Finefrock, Attorney Alaine Grbach, Attorney Richard Puleo, Attorney Clifford Reider,

Chris and Kelly Coran, Pastor Louis and first lady Katy Butcher, Bishop Malven and Apostle Marvel Stutter, and my uncle Reverend Willie and Aunt Corren Stallworth. Also to the men who took me under their wing and raised me to preach the gospel Reverend Anthony W. Baker Presiding. ELD, Reverend Willie and Francis Morant, The Late Ira Shank, Dave from Tristate, Ben CSR. My friends Pastor Yvette Withfield, Andrew Marshall, and Lou and Pam Bazella

I want to thank all my family and friends for their many prayers, financial support and encouragement.For without their help this book would not be possible. Special thanks to my Executive Secretary Lora Pennington for all her help typing and proof reading this more than once.

CONTENTS

v

ACKNOWLEDGMENTS

This book is inspired by my Lord and Savior Jesus Christ. First let me thank God for allowing me to write this book. It was very difficult at first, but because so many of my friends kept encouraging me to tell My Life Story. They would say, Reverend Shell you should not die and let all that you experienced not be told. That inspired me to write this book; my prayer is that this book will help someone as they journey through life.

~My Parents~

"Honour thy father and mother: that thy days may be long upon the land which the Lord thy God giveth thee."
Exodus 20:12

I was born to Ofield and Alice Shell on January 8, 1952 in Freemanville, Alabama at home because back then black women did not go to the hospital to have a baby. They had mid wives that would come to the house and deliver the baby. My father was an ordinary black man and raised by a single parent. He did not have a lot of education but he was smart enough as so not to work as a farmer. He would leave home and go look for construction work. There were very few black men that would leave their families to find better work to provide a better life for them. He would return every weekend. He was not very religious but he loved the Lord. My father is greatly missed.

My mother Alice was the back bone of the family. She had a ninth grade education that would transfer into a four year college degree today. She was a mother, teacher, business woman. She did a little bit of everything. She worked in restaurants, took in laundry, sold the vegetables, homemade butter and buttermilk and even a little moonshine. But most of all she loved the Lord. She would always say "With the Lord on your side there's nothing you can't accomplish." She used to tell us to believe in yourself, hold yourself up, even when you may not have the best, what you have keep it up. She would tell me "Son, brother may have and sister may have but God bless the child that has his own." My mother had so much respect and was so respected by the community that she could send her children to any business she dealt with and tell them to let them have this and they would because my mother's word meant something. She would tell me, son "Let your word mean something, for your word is better than money." The one thing I love about my mother is she always said "Son whatever you do be persistent."

For Mother Day 1997, my sister Belinda put together a booklet honoring our mother. In it she wrote,

"This booklet is written in honor of our mother, Mrs. Alice Stallworth Shell. Mother was born on April 30, 1922. She is the Mother of eleven children and is a strong woman. Mother believes in the Almighty God; the Creator of the heavens and the earth; the God who sent His Son, Jesus Christ, into the world to die for her sins. And today, I truly thank God for Mother, and I honor her with this booklet. And most of all, I thank

Mother for making her God my God. For it was not by words alone that she influenced my life, but by what she demonstrated in her daily life style, Today I appreciate the stand Mother took for whatever she believed in, if she thought it to be correct. Mother always tried to live, to the best of her knowledge, a Christian life. She truly desired a pure heart; a heart free of guile. Yes, Mother made some mistakes, when she was up and about, even in instructing her children. However, if she really understood something to be wrong, according to the Word of God, Mother did not do it; nor would she partake in wrong doings, even if it left her standing alone. Mother was not a pretender. One of her most famous sayings was, 'Don't pretend, just be who or what you are.' From her heart, Mother attempted to lead, guide and direct her children in the way they should go. Because of Mother's honest desire to please God, we are where we are today. You see Mother's greatest desire was not that she obtains riches, but that she would have eternal life. Not only did she desire eternal life for herself, but also for her children. And today God is still answering Mother's prayers."

Know that as I embark on this journey, one that I am about to share with you, I pray and hope that it will inspire you and help you in your journey. Through all my trials and tribulations I must tell you to be persistent.

~From Alabama to New York~

*"And labour, working with our own hands:
being reviled, we bless; being persecuted,
we suffer it:
1 Corinthian's 4:12*

As you know my name is Willie E Shell Sr. I was born to Ofield and Alice Shell. I grew up in Freemanville, Alabama. I attended the Freemanville Elementary school until I was old enough to go to high school in Atmore Alabama. I did not just drop out of school. What happen at the age of fifteen and a half, I was offered a job in Kingston, North Carolina. It was a summer job harvesting tobacco for a man named Peter from Freemanville. My mother and father knew him. It was his business and he would get people to work during the summer harvesting crops. When Mr. Peter asked my mother if she would let me go, my mother told him that I was afraid of worms. I also explained to Mr. Peter that I was afraid of worms. Mr. Peter assured my mother and me that I would be the tractor driver. So my mother let me go work for Mr. Peter.

After arriving in Kingston North Carolina, it rained for seven days. When it finally stopped raining it was late in the season and Mr. Peter needed all the men young and old to work the ground and harvest the tobacco crops. At which time I reminded Mr. Peter that he had given his word to my mother and father that I would be a tractor driver. Mr. Peter assured me that there were no worms on the tobacco. I said "alright." He removed me from the tractor and put me in the field pulling the tobacco. I was doing ok until I looked up and saw all the worms. When I stopped running I was on the highway, remember I was only fifteen and a half years old. I then told Mr. Peter that I could not go back out there and he told me that if I don't go back in the field that I would have to leave the farm. At which time I called my mother who in turn called my brother Andrew and my brother Roosevelt. Both of whom lived in New York. I did not know that they even knew where I was at. Early that Saturday morning my brother showed up and said mother said for us to come get you. That's how I got from Alabama to New York.

At the age of fifteen and a half I was not old enough to get a job. My brother Andrew was a truck driver and made deliveries too many companies and warehouses. He knew of this one company that was hiring and he talked to them and they offered me a job. I worked there until I was 18. My mother and brothers never asked me "Don't you want to go back and finish high school?" My brother Roosevelt took me under his wing because he was an entrepreneur. He had ice cream truck, he drove a taxi, and he also ran a vegetable stand. He and I used to go to the Apollo for amateur night; we won karaoke at the bar. Learning from my mother along with watching and being taught by my brother. I learned how to make money and became an entrepreneur after two and a half years under my brother's wing.

~Elizabeth~

"Whoso findeth a wife findeth a good thing, and obtaineth favour of the Lord."
Proverbs 18:22

At the age of eighteen, I moved to Lancaster Pennsylvania. There I met the love of my life Elizabeth Cummings, the soon to be Elizabeth Shell. She was born to Clifford and Beatrice Cummings. Elizabeth and I married on November 3, 1970. The Lord blessed us to raise three sons, Willie Jr, David, and Terrence. During this time Elizabeth also helped raise my younger brother Winston and Niece Altamese. Elizabeth was first a wife who loved her husband then a mother who loved her three sons. She was a strong woman, she not only loved me and her sons, but she loved her family.

I remember in 1973 my mother came to visit us for two weeks. My mother had so much knowledge and wisdom and she knew Elizabeth and I were having marital problems. She convinced her not to leave me. He is my son and he is going to make you a good husband. What Elizabeth did not know was that when my mother left I was leaving. I called my uncle Willie Stallworth and asked him if I could come and live with him and my aunt Corren. He said "come on." I left Lancaster and moved to Columbia, South Carolina with my aunt and uncle. Little did I know that my wife was in contact with my uncle? Neither did I know that when I made that decision that I would have to attend church every Sunday.

After five months, one Friday evening low and behold my wife showed up. I said to my uncle, "Did you know that Elizabeth was coming." His response was "yes." Why did you not tell me? He replied "she asked me not too tell you. Elizabeth stayed that weekend. I asked who was taken care of Willie Jr. She said I left him with my parents. She left that Monday to return back to Lancaster. During those six months, I had dedicated my life to the Lord. My uncle and Aunt encouraged me to return back to Lancaster to my wife and son. I left Columbia, South Carolina and went back to my family. In January Elizabeth had our second son.

Not only was Elizabeth a mother and wife, she was also a good example for her sons. I remember when she signed Willie jr up for piano lessons, not only did he play but she taught herself also in order to teach him that if she can learn he can too. Elizabeth was a strong woman. Her and my sister Mary would load up the boys and my niece Altamese and take off to Alabama and say I'll call you when I get there. She also was somewhat of a freelance photographer. She loved taken pictures of everything. She hung her pictures all over the house and was changing them with each new picture she took.

~Learning to Listen and Trust God~

"Trust in the Lord with all thine heart; and lean not unto thine own understanding. In all thy ways acknowledge him, and he shall direct thy paths."
Proverbs 3:5-6

After returning to Lancaster, I continued to go to church. But I fell by the waist side. My uncle had always said "son if you fall, don't fall below your knees." Upon returning to Lancaster in November 1973 I was able to get a job at Bunner Corporation. I worked there until April 1974. At which time I left and got a job at Armstrong World Industries, after being there for six to eight months I was approached by Reverend T.C. Gillespie to come and try out with his gospel group. I said what is the name of your group? He responded The Golden Tone of Lancaster. Not only did I make the group but I became the manager. I was blessed to manage that group from 1976 to 1981.

After joining the group, I again rededicated my life to the Lord. If you want to know what kind of friends you have just say I've turned my life over to the Lord. I thought I had two friends that would be happy for me. Instead they became so ugly to the point they wouldn't even speak to me.

I remember my family and my wife, we were returning home from a funeral in Alabama following my brother. The fog was so thick you could cut it with your knife. My wife was driving and I was asleep in the back seat, they had to stop and get gas. It is a good thing to have a relationship with the Lord, because he spoke to me and told me to tell my family to stay put. But my brother lives in Brooklyn New York and they had to get back to work. I responded OK. So we all decided to disobey warning from God and leave the place we were. We had just refilled. You see it pays to listen to God when he speaks to you. After pulling out from the service station we weren't two miles down the road when we became a part of sixty nine car and truck pile up. Thank God no one was hurt. My car was totaled, but thanks to the Lord and Savior Jesus Christ we were all safe. We only lost one car in that accident and it had to be mine. It was a lesson learned for me to not only to listen when he speaks but also obey him.

After that accident we were able to pile in my brothers vehicles and they drove us home. That left my wife and I without transportation. I needed a ride to work and against my better judgment called a gentleman that I knew resented me for turning my life over to the

Lord. What I did not realize was how much he hated me. He and I worked the same shift. I remember calling him and telling him about the accident and asked him to pick me up and I would pay him for the ride. I just need a ride for about two weeks until I could get another car. That Sunday night started my work week and I called him and said don't forget me. I called him at nine that evening to make sure he did not forget me. I knew he resented my walk with the Lord but for the money he would pick me up.

He would not even give me a ride for the money. I waited till ten thirty and my wife said he was not coming to pick me up. So I began to walk. When I got to work he was there. From that day to the present I never asked him what was wrong. I already knew that they hated my walk with the Lord.

The Lord blessed me to get a Ford car. It was green with a vinyl top. The body looked good but the top was all sun blistered. I was so embarrassed. Not only about the car, but also about the fact that I had only one suite to wear to church every Sunday.

~Growing in Faith~

"Now faith is the substance of things hoped for, the evidence of things not seen"
Hebrews 11:1

In May 1974, a women, minister pastor named Agnes Brook was sent to pastor at St. Paul AUFCMP church. Reverend Brook was the first pastor I ever heard speak about faith and tithe. After settling under her Ministry, she taught me and my wife about faith and tithe.

In 1977 Rev. Brook left the conference and went independent. Not only did she leave the conference but she moved right next to my wife and me. My wife and I were very young; my sister Arbra led us to Saint Paul's church. We did not want to leave so we stayed. Then they wanted me to become a deacon. I agreed as long as it does not interfere with my time with my gospel group. That church then split and went independent.

Being a deacon I had the opportunity to meet the bishop and the presiding elder and talk about what was happening. I remember the old men and women said "We need to have a meeting with the bishop and the presiding elder." So I said "were can we have the meeting." They all said "at you and Sister Elizabeth's house." We were very young in our twenties. We looked at each other and said alright. If you want to hold it at our house that's alright with us. Well the next thing we know we went from the meeting to church every Sunday in our home. My wife and I had to move furniture around every Saturday night and set up chairs for the Sunday service. That went on from 1978 to 1980.

During that time, I was still manager of the gospel group and we were meeting in my basement every Saturday afternoon at three o'clock. I was still working at Armstrong, running the hauling business I had started in 1974 and was keeping my faith in the Lord strong. I could see God manifest his spirit right in front of me. Rev. Brook taught faith and tithe. She would say pay your tithe and see "If I will not open you the windows o heaven, and pour you out a blessing, that there shall not be room enough to receive it." (Malachi 3:10) October 1975 my wife and I took her at her word and started paying our tithe and obeying God's word. We put our trust in the Lord more and more.

We still had that green Ford with the sun blistered vinyl roof, it was very embarrassing, but I remember what my mother told me, "Son you may not have the best, but take care of what you do have." All the guys in the group had very nice cars. Some had new cars and here I was the manager with the ugliest car in the group. I kept paying my tithe and being obedient to God's word. I knew I could not get a car on credit because I messed up my credit before I rededicated my life back to the Lord. My wife and I had been working very hard to fix our credit. Armstrong had what you call a bank loan program. If you work there for more than 6 months you could apply through them for a bank loan. It was not a guarantee but because I worked at Armstrong you would think that would carry some weight, but it didn't.

I remember it like it was yesterday. I bought the application home and on Monday filled it out. We prayed over the application and returned it to the front office. They said you should hear from the bank within twenty four hours. That's when my faith had to take hold. I went car shopping before I even got the loan. Twenty four hours later, still no phone call. Thursday I was standing on my steps and I saw the mail man three doors away from my house and he had a letter in his hand. I knew it was from the bank and it was a letter to let me know that my loan request had been denied. I could do nothing but look up and say "Lord why." At that point the Holy Spirit hit me and the next thing I knew I was at the bank door. The manager met me at the door. I did not say a word, he said "I know why you are here. Here is my card attach it to the application and send it back through." I took his card and did what he said. I attached the card to the application the very same day that was a Thursday. That Monday I received a call from the bank to tell me my loan had been approved. We had searched for a car and ended up purchasing a Buick.

In 1975 we moved to Terrace Road. The house was small and very hot in the summer and cold in the winter. The windows were so small that you could not even put a fan in them. I slept in the basement that summer because it was cooler down there. There was one big heating vent in the middle of the first floor hallway which did not warm very much of the house. Through our faith and obedience, and again knowing our credit was not good. But we had a ton of faith. So we began to trust and believe God to help us purchase a home. The clean out and hauling business was good. It has been about one year now with this business under our belt. Both my wife and I had good jobs. Because of my business I had put an ad in the paper and I began doing work for many realtors.

One day I was doing some work for a realtor and we were talking, I said to her "Pat I would like to buy a house." She said "I can help you with that." She asked "how is your credit?" I said "not good." So she said "let me take you and Elizabeth around and show you some houses." She did but to no avail, due to the fact she was showing us all row houses. There were certain areas for certain people, even in the 7th ward. She took us to places on Christian and Green Street over by the Bean Cafe on Stevens Street. That area had been nothing but row homes. I said to Pat no need to show us anymore row homes, you must have some semidetached homes. The same day we were riding down South Marshall Street heading toward East End Avenue and I said "Look Pat, what's wrong with that house?" She replied "Nothing I don't think you can afford it." I asked her what they are asking for it. She said it just went on the market and listing for $19,600.00. I said let's go for it. This was January 1976. We started working on it because of our credit. We had thing's to work through. But we did not give up. We were persistent.

I was working hard with my hauling and clean out business and at Armstrong. We got our credit straightened out. Thank God for our friend Pat. Due to the hauler business and going to the landfill every day I would come home with a pocket full of change and dump it in our piggy bank. June 30, 1976 we made settlement on our house. It was a Friday. We thought we had enough money in the bank to cover the check we gave the mortgage company. Saturday morning we get a call from the bank saying Mr. Shell you need $285.00 to cover that check you gave the mortgage company. I looked at my wife and asked what we are going to do. We agreed to open the piggy bank and see how much was in there. We set down and counted it out. To our surprise we had saved $280.00. We rolled it and took it to the bank and that same day we moved into our house. That's what tithe, faith and obedience will do for you. It will give you faith in God and God will give you faith in people. When I say favor I talk about the kind between man and women.

After moving into our house on South Marshall Street and managing the gospel group from 1976 to 1980. In 1978 we were meeting for rehearsals at the Franklin Community Center. During one meeting the committee person came to the group and said you have to move your meeting. The group asked me where we were going. I said if anyone one knows where we could go let me know. They all looked at me and said what about your basement? I responded, I have to talk to my wife remember we already have the one responsibility of having church at our house on Sunday. We had to rearrange the furniture on Saturday night and put it back Sunday afternoon. When I asked Elizabeth said that it is up to you if you want the group to meet here until you can find a building. Again when you pay your tithe and be obedient to God's word, favor will follow you. The Lord blessed that group also. He allowed us to be on the stage with some of the top gospel singers such as Mighty Clouds of Joy, Willie, Neal Johnson, and The Gospel

Key Note, Shirley Cease, and many more.

In 1980 the group decided to go their separate ways. I asked my wife what happen to me, after the group went their separate ways I was still a deacon of the church, teaching Sunday school, Bible study and singing in the choir. The Lord was moving me from the stage to the pulpit. Things were happening so fast.

~Serving the Lord Together~

"And if it seem evil unto you to serve the Lord, choose you this day whom ye will serve; whether the gods which your fathers served that were on the other side of the flood, or the gods of the Amorites, in whose land ye dwell; but as for me and my house, we will serve the Lord.
Joshua 24:15

As I close this chapter of my life, I am trusting God to help write the next chapter. As I try to write this story, it is very hard for me. This is the story of my life with the love of my life. Who I miss every day and so as I begin to share the story of my wife and I, let me give you some back ground on her.

I had given you a little background on my beautiful wife earlier. Now it's time for you to get to know this wonderful woman even better. Elizabeth Cummings was born to Clifford and Beatrice Cummings on December 24, 1951 at Lancaster General Hospital in Lancaster, Pennsylvania. She attended McCaskey High School, but left high school in 1970 because she was pregnant with our first child, Willie Junior. We got married November 30, 1970. Elizabeth reminded me a lot of my mother.

Her first job was at Hubler Toy Factory. Being young and not knowing what I wanted to do, I went from job to job during the next three years of our marriage. I worked three months at RCA, Grinnell Foundry and the last job I had was Ankle Continental in Columbia South Carolina with my uncle Willie and Aunt Corrine.

Elizabeth had three jobs. As I stated earlier she worked at Hubler Toy Factory, she quit there and went to work for Slay Maker Lock, and she was laid off from that job December 19, 1974. That year we would move from Mulberry Street to Terrace Road. Elizabeth took advantage of being laid off, using her free time to enjoy the family and her life. Our second son David was born January 20, 1974. After her eight weeks she returned to work.

During the year 1974 our life turned completely around. That was when God really began to bring us unto him and make us a team. In 1974 I rededicated my life back to the Lord. Elizabeth also rededicated her life to the Lord. As I stated earlier we were living on Terrace Road and we had the Rev Agnes A Brooks teaching on Titan Faith.

Elizabeth was working at Slay Maker Lock and I was working at Armstrong World Industries plus had my part time hauler and clean out business on the side. Again my friend Pat who was a realtor, read my ad in the paper and asked me if I could help with a house clean out. I responded yes, that was the beginning of how God moved into our life. After that job Pat was so impressed with my work that she said "I am going to let every realtor know about you." She did just that. My business was growing.

During the fall of 1975, when things were at a turning point in our lives we had bought into Rev Brooks teaching especially on tithing coming from Malachi 3:8-12. I will explain these verses as I go through mine and Elizabeth's journey. Verse 8-12 states "Will a man rob God, yet you rob me. But you say, wherein have we robbed thee? In tithes and offerings. Ye are cursed with a curse: for ye have robbed me, even this whole nation. Bring ye all the tithes into the storehouse, that there may be meat in mine house, and prove me mow herewith saith the Lord of hosts, If I will not open you the windows of heaven, and pour you out a blessing, that there shall not be room enough to receive it. And I will rebuke the devourer for your sakes, and he shall not destroy the fruits of your ground; neither shall your vine cast her fruit before the time in the field, saith the Lord of hosts. And all nations shall call you blessed: for ye shall be a delightsome land, saith the Lord of hosts."

We were in church every Sunday. The Lord had blessed us with a Green vinyl blistered Ford car and a Blue truck. The truck looked better than the green car. Elizabeth never complained she just drove the car around during the week and on Sunday I would be the one to drive us around

In July 1976 we moved into the South Marshall Street house. Then September 5, 1976 our third son Terrence was born. My wife and I decided to settle down and focus on raising our children and being faithful to the Lord. In 1978 another property at 72 South Marshall Street came up for sale through the bank. I came home and told my wife that the corner property was for sale. I said I would like to look at it and she said we don't have any money. I was the only one working. I called the bank and inquired about the property. We set up a day and time to go look at it. We met the man from the bank who showed us the whole building including the small building in the back. I asked him what the bank was asking for it and he said I had to make an offer. We did not know what that meant. I went to see Ira Shank, who was a Realty State Agent. I was doing lots of work for Mr. Shank. He helped me and Elizabeth. I put the offer in for 19,000.00. The man from the bank called and asked us to come to his office. We met with him and he said they had higher offers then yours but that because we lived in the neighborhood they were giving the property to us. We said thank you for that and left the bank, before we reached the elevator my wife asked me how we were going to get the money. I said God will make a way.

For about two weeks I was working hard and praying. Then one day the Lord spoke to me and told me to go talk to Ira Shank and explain my problem to him. He asked that we meet him at the building the next day. That same day he told me he would take care of this for us. He went and purchased the building for us. He did not charge us one dime. In Malachi Chapter 3 verse 10 and he said test me in this, Says the Lord Almighty," and see if I will not throw open the floodgates of heaven and pour so much blessing that you will not have room for it. After we got the building Elizabeth asked what are we going to do with it?   We decided to open a restaurant; again we had no money and not so good credit. Because the building was not in our name we could not get a loan on it. The bank required you put at least twenty percent down. We were opening a business with two people who had no business experience. I had this friend who worked at Armstrong and was a self-made business man.   He owned mainly property in the city. I also had done some work for him. I told him that Elizabeth and I wanted to start a restaurant and we needed 2,000.00 and the bank would give us the rest. At no point in time did I think to ask him for the money. His word was is that all you need to get going? I said yes. He gave me his address and said to come by his house tomorrow and there would be a bag behind the milk box.   That morning I went to the address and there was the bag with 2,000.00 in it. He never asked for any interest. That was a reminder of what my mother told me, "Trust me son your word is worth more than money."   After praying the bank granted us the loan I knew it pays to follow God when he is leading you.

We needed to have the building remodeled and

bought up to code for the restaurant. We started getting estimates on the cost. We had ninety days. One contractor said he could have us open in two weeks and his bid was low. The second contractor was a black man who pleaded with us to please give him a chance. He showed me pictures of some work he had done. I told him the other contractor was lower and said he could have us open in two weeks. Because you need a chance and you need to put this kind of business in your resume we will give you a chance. I told him he had one month. Well when you don't follow God who is leading you suffer. I ended up doing the work myself. Let me just say while doing all this my wife and I were still raising our three sons, I was still working at Armstrong and doing the hauler and clean out business. We still had church in our house every Sunday and rehearsal in our basement for the gospel group, and traveling every Saturday and Sunday evening doing gospel programs.

In 1979 my brother Winston came to live with us. We were now raising four boys, our three sons Willie Jr, David, Terrence and my brother Winston. It became too much and I knew something had to give soon. We decided to rent out the restaurant. After renting that out Elizabeth decided to go back to school to get her diploma. After receiving that she decided to take some English classes at Millersville. The boys were now in Middle and High school and the restaurant was rented out. Elizabeth decided to take on a part time job while still being a mom/wife. This lasted for about a year and a half.

In September 1980 our lives took another turn. The Lord called me to preach the gospel.
In June 1981 I preached my trial sermon.

In 1982 I decided to return to school to get my diploma. After receiving my diploma I attended Lancaster Bible College. It was mandatory that you attend AUFCMP School of religion. From 1981-1984 I was assistant Pastor at many AUFCMP churches. In 1984 I received my first pastor charge and Elizabeth and I were sent to Pastor a church in Mardela Spring Maryland. That church was one hundred and seventy five miles from our house. I remember returning from a conference on Sunday and was told if you are not happy with the charge you could come back on Wednesday for a new charge. Thanks to my fellow brother and sister the late Rev Julie Gomez and Rev Andrew Jenkin I was happy with the charge to go to Star Bethlehem, Delaware. I was an Associate Pastor to start in Bethlehem, Delaware. They talked me into going to a reconvene conference that was held on Wednesday. I said ok as long as I don't have to do any driving. They all agreed and bought me lunch. We were off to Delaware where the reconvene conference was being held. When we got there I went up to the second floor and fell asleep. Little did I know that there was a plan for me. The plan was for me and my wife to hit the road Pastoring. That day, just as the conference was over, I heard my name. Rev Shell come down here, I am sending you and Sister Elizabeth to Mardela Springs Maryland. My next question was where is that? Off Highway 13 they stated. Where is highway 13? You were sitting by some of the members; ask them the best way to get there.

When I returned home my wife was not happy. She asked where that was and I told her I did not know. All I was told was that it is on Highway 13 about two and a half hours from Delaware, which meant about three and a half hours from Lancaster. It was a long way to go and Pastor. That Sunday we got up at 3 am to get everyone ready for the long drive ahead. Church service was to start at 9 am and at 8:45am we were still driving not knowing where we were. We were on Highway 13. I remember stopping at a McDonalds and asked someone if they knew were exactly the church was. One lady said yes she passes it every day coming to work. She said stay on Highway 13 till you come to 7 make a right on 7, take that to 50 make a right the church is about 2 miles down that road. I asked about how many more miles and she about 15. From here it is now 9am. I got back in the car and told Elizabeth how much farther it was, I said I don't want to be disobedient and I know if I don't take this charge I might not get another one but if it is any further than 15 miles we are going home. This is not God's doing. Low and behold it was exactly 15 miles from that McDonalds to the church. We arrived at 9:15am. We were tired and sleepy but we pushed ourselves. I had the hardest time because I had to preach.

There were only twelve adults and one child sitting there waiting on us. I went on and did what I was sent to do. After the worship service I was asked to have a finance meeting. I went alone with the trustee and secretary. After a prayer the secretary said Rev we don't know why the bishop sent you and your family all the way down here, we don't have money to pay you. We cannot even pay for your gas. She showed me the books and they were only taken in about $25.00 to $30.00 a week. I could not say anything but my Lord. During the meeting I said let's just pray about this all week. Only thing they had going for them was a three bedroom house for the Pastor and his family to live in. That was a plus. The family loved it and the boys seen it as a way to get out of Lancaster every weekend. The next week my wife was packing the car up with everything you would need for camping, sheets, blanket, pillows and Sunday clothes. When I got there the next Sunday morning I said I don't know why the Bishop and the Presiding Elder sent me and my family here, all I can ask is that you follow my wife and I as we follow Christ. What they did not know was that we were tithes. From that Sunday on the church went from taking in $25.00-$30.00 on Sunday to making $400.00- $500.00 per Sunday.

The word got around that Mardela Springs has a new Pastor in town. This one member had a son who was very abusive to her. Every Saturday she would wait for my family to arrive. Before we could get out of the car she would be there in tears. Every Saturday she would come to the pulpit and pray to God for help for her son. But there was never any change. I explained to her that he needs to do this for himself. The next Saturday I went to see this young man and talk to him. I said to him I know you don't know me but I know you from your mother. I don't like what you are doing to your mother. God sent me here to extend an invitation to you. This is not a way a child should treat his mother. This Sunday we are taking you to the altar and leaving you there so that Lord can heal you. I suggest you meet us there. He replied, I don't know. That Sunday night he was hit by a truck and died. He was my first funeral service. What a service it was, people came from all over because the family was well known. The church was full, the dining room was full, people were standing around outside. I can still see this to this day. I was nervous. The pulpit was filled with Ministers and Pastors. My Presiding

Elder was there to cheer me on. My wife was there with that smile on her face saying you can do this. Just to tell you what Jesus said is true "great is he that is in me then he that in the world." (John 4:4)

As you read again this verse from Malachi 3:10 let me take you back to the beginning when I told my wife that this was not God doing and I don't know why the man I look up to would do me like this. It reminds me of Josephs brother how they sold him into slavery. I felt that he had betrayed me and my wife and for unknown reasons. But that also reminds me of what Isaiah said in Isaiah 54:17 "No weapon form against you shall property." From that funeral service just as in Malachi 3:10, He said test me in this, "Saith the Lord of hosts" and see if I will not throw open the floodgates of heaven and pour so much blessing that you will not have room for it.

From that funeral service the floodgates of heaven were open to me and my family. I began preaching two to three sermons every Sunday. I precisely remember this one service I was asked to preach. It was a little town way back in the woods. It was my Pastor Stude home church. I said ok. Well, little did I know that the church would seat 800-1,000 people. As we approached the church, I started to look around. I noticed all these high class cars from, New York, New Jersey and Virginia. My wife was sitting in the passenger seat just looking at me with that smile saying you can do this. When I got to the church my Pastor Stude came and took me to meet the Pastor there. Because I was still young the Pastor took me by the hand and settled me down son you're going to be alright. What a blessing that was. Another one where he said test me in this, "Saith the Lord of hosts" and see if I will not throw open the floodgates of heaven and pour so much blessing that you will not have room for it. That evening the church took in three big baskets of money. So much my wife could barely fit it in her big purse. Not only that but the Lord had opened a door for us, from the East Shore to Delaware whenever we stopped along the highway people would know who we were. You are the Shell family and we would eat for free. I don't know how but somehow I ended up on the radio. My wife and I received blessings from some of the members of this church up until 1995. The conference moved us from this church. On our last visit we shared with them that our children were grown and now journeying through this world as adults. As of this date I still make trips to visit.

In 1984 the next confer year they sent us to Pastor St Paul Church here in Lancaster, Pa. My wife and I pastored here from 1985 to 1988. The presiding Bishop Robert Water passed away in 1987. After his death Rev Delbert Jackson, who was Bishop elected, and upon the Presiding Bishop's death automatically become presiding Bishop. That's when all hell broke loose in that conference. Mr. Jackson not only wanted control but he wanted all church to be deeds to that conference. This destroyed many churches that were not in the conference. As I write this story about my involvement and pastor in the AMUFCMPC I am told there is still a legal battle going on in the court twenty plus years later.

In 1988, my wife and I were sent to pastor Trinity AUFCMPH in Zion Maryland. During that year I had a profitable conference. In 1989 I was sent back for another year but I didn't finish that term. This would have ended May 1990. In 1989 after my wife and I return to Trinity AUFCMPH for the second year there arose a financial problem in the church. I called Mr. Jackson and said we request your presence. He said write me a letter requesting the Bishop and presiding Elder at your next meeting. I did that and the man came to the next meeting and talked for 45 minutes. Never once said one thing about the purposed he was here for. After he finished talking he said let's all stand. I said Lord I don't believe what I just heard and witnessed. I'll never forget it. I remember like it was yesterday. I grabbed his case and walked him to his car. I was still so angry I did not know what to say. All I could say to him was "I can't believe you did this." He opened his brief case took a $100.00 bill out and gave it to me and said forget it. I took the $100.00 bill balled it up in my hand and threw it in his car and said get the hell out of here for I am not for sale. Well three days later I received a letter from Mr. Jackson saying Rev Willie and Elizabeth Shell, you are no longer Pastor of the Trinity AUFCMPC church and you're no longer AUFCMPC conference members. That ended an affiliation with the AUMPFC conference. That is when we decided to return to our home church.

Well low and behold all hell broke loose a month later. I was at a service when a court order came in saying I was being sued to turn the church over to the conference. I said it was not my church. It belongs to the people. I was only the chairmen and singing along with the others when the building was purchased. If the people want to deed it, that's fine by me. About eighty percent of the people said NO. The conference did not give us one dime when we purchased this building. Now that it's paid for they want it. Well here we go again. My wife and I got pulled into this legal battle, one that we never asked for. The next thing we knew a few months later I was pulled into court. The court split the times up, the group I was pastoring had the building Monday, Tuesday Wednesday and Sunday till 12:30pm. That went on until 1997. After that the court gave the building over to the conference. I was hurt and so were the members. I felt that God had let them down. So I started looking around for about three months. We held service in the lunch room in my office. In 1997 the Lord blessed us to be able to rent from the Presbyterian Church located on South Queen Street. That worked out for the good; there service was from 9:30am to 10:30am. So we did not have to change our times. We had a key and all we had to do was lock up when we were done. We were there until March 2000, when the members merged with Brightside Baptist Church. During this time we were still raising our boys; my oldest one had graduated from high school with a 3.0 grade point average. We tried hard to convince him to go to college but the street had much more to offer so off he went. As I close this chapter that runs from 1989-2000 at the same time another chapter begins to unfold.

~The Test of Time~

"Thou therefore endure hardness, as a good soldier of Jesus Christ"
2 Timothy 2:3

We are moving into the 21th century and as I reveal the life of my wife and I you can see it brought with it many challenges, from depression time, faith time, family time to modern day slavery and oppression. The 1990's took us into many trials and tribulations. During that time we were still raising three boys plus looking after my in laws.

In 1990 the Federal Government mandated that all states must put in place a recycling program to reduce landfill space. My wife and I had been in the hauling business since 1974. In 1991 The Lord had given me a vision and said build a one stop recycle center. The first building we went to was on North Street it was for rent. I called the landlord and talked with him telling him what I wanted to do with it and he said ok. Two weeks later I received a call from him saying the neighbors were going to oppose it. I decided to have a community meeting and explain to the neighbors what our plan was and see if we could sell them on it. This one black fellow sat there and did not say a word, the next week at the city zoning meeting there was that black man who was against us. We were told that we could appeal it, and we said no. If the Lord wants us to have a recycling center he will provide.

In 1991 I was driving down South Franklin Street, when I came passed a building for rent. I called the owner to inquire about it, we came to an agreement and he rented me the place. A few months later he decided to sell the place plus he had two lots to go with it. I said Lord you know how to do it. In 1992 the Late James (Jim) Hyson was bought back here from California by the former Mayor Janice Stoke to recruit minorities that wanted to start their own business. The Lancaster Chamber was also looking to help in the minority community. They had hired Mr. Derrick Steven. Derrick had heard that we wanted to put a laundromat where the restaurant once was. I remember this short black brother came knocking at our door and said "I was told that I should come see you and Elizabeth. I work for the Lancaster Chamber and we are helping minorities start a new business. I was told that you want to build a laundromat. We said yes and he said "I believe we can help you." At the same time we were still working with Jim Hyson to get the recycling center going.

Thanks to former City Councilmen and former County Commissioner Ron Ford who helped us get the pass to start a recycling center. After getting through zoning we worked hard on our business plan. We completed the business plan in 1993. After we completed the business plan Jim said to me "Willie I got to be up front with you." I looked at Jim and said "what are you trying to say?" He said they will not let you have this business in this city." I responded "Jim why are you saying that?" He replied it is too big of a business for a black man, I replied to Jim "The Lord said greater is he that in me then he that in the world." Jim and I worked very hard. After the business plan was complete, we started seeking loans from the City of Lancaster that had a program with the state where they would submit the application on your behalf and the state would give them a grant and the city would in turn loan it to you at a low interest rate.

When I started this business in 1995 we met all the zoning boards' requirements as a small business. This was done with a lot of hard work and no government help. As I stated before, I did not know that the mayor and the administrators were moving toward a one hauler system and this same administration was requesting minorities to help start new businesses in the city.

On July 11, 1995 my wife Elizabeth and I held the ground breaking ceremony after completing and going through all the requirements. After meeting all the administrative requirements, I learned that the mayor had another agenda and that was to take the city to a one hauler system. So she started to derail my wife and my plan. That same year the city received a grant from Enterprise Zone loan. Because Mr. and Mrs. Shell were both graduates of the city's business planning and mentorship program (BPMP) which helped city residents in the planning of a new and expanding business, made us eligible for a low interest loan from the city sponsored by Pride Loan Fund. In May of 1995 the city received a grant from the state to re loam to us. Our plan was to hold a loan ceremony, just as we had held a ground breaking ceremony.

That grant was handed down to the city. In May of

1994 we also submitted an application to the Pennsylvania Minority Business Development Authority. Later that same year, we received a letter from the Authority that our loan had been approved. After we received that letter, we contacted the Mayor and said we would like to have a one-time settlement with the city and Pennsylvania Minority Business Development. The Mayor refused and said she did not want any part of it. I did not know what to think. I asked Jim what was going on here. He replied "Willie I don't know, the Mayor wouldn't talk to me." I called my attorney to explain things to him. I then called the attorney from Pennsylvania Minority Business and explained to them what was going on. They said we can have a meeting at your attorney's office and they explained the plan to us. In December 1995 the Mayor who was sitting on the grant that the city had received from the state to re-loan for a startup of a small business, called me and said we needed to close this loan by the end of the month or the money will be returned to the state. The Mayor had been sitting on the loan from May 1995 to the last week of December 1995. We were already 18months behind schedule. That same year in May 1995 my mentor Jim

Hyson passed away unexpected. My wife and I were visiting family in New York when we got the news that Jim had passed. We could not believe it that really hurt us. Jim was our leader. He knew his way around and who to talk too.

After his death, I learned the Mayor wanted to take the city to a one hauler system. That's when all our trouble started. We were left with no one to lead us. We did not know who to trust or who to talk too. One day our friend Derrick Steven who had worked with us getting the laundromat together stepped up to the plate and said "I am here for you all" and brother has he been there and is still there for me to this day.

In 1996 there were twenty six independent haulers in the city of Lancaster, half of them were minorities and only one had a recycling center. Today I am the only black hauler on the east coast with a recycling center. The city used their governmental powers against these minority businessmen to drive them out of business. They were afraid to get into their trucks, because they knew that they were going to be harassed by the police and given fines. Some haulers lost their families and everything they had. I managed to survive only by the grace of God.

Now the New Year was here. We could start somewhere in April of 1996 which put us two years behind. As we were working with the contractor, another recycling center was moving into the city and was ready to start operating in six weeks. The man who was put in that recycling center called me and said "Willie can you come down to my facility. I would like to show you something." I said I would stop by the next day. I called to make sure he was there and I called a friend of mine Keith Holland and asked him to go with me to meet Dixon from Brandywine Recycling. He said yes. He went with me to meet this man where he showed us his large blue print of his operation and offered to fly us to Florida were it was being made for one week. Then he said to me "Willie why don't you scrap your plan and come manage this place for me." I responded, "Sir, thank you but I don't want to commit to working for someone else. If I want to work for someone else, I would have stayed at Armstrong and I believe there is enough recycling material for both of us."

We knew that in order to compete with Dixon Recycling, we needed to implement phase 1 and 2. Together we knew we only had enough money for phase 1. Construction began on phase one and boy was it hard. That year was a trying time, we had a homemade recycling box, a down stroke baler and the contractor had to stop work on the building because we ran out of money. That got put on hold for some time. We had three employees; we were taking recycling from small haulers because everything was done manually. My wife ran the office, and the recycling center. I ran the hauler business during the day and big truck at night. It was hard. Then in 1997 the late Billy Joe Herr was running for Mayor. She came to me and said "Willie I heard you need more money to finish your operation." I said yes. She said "You know I am running for Mayor." I responded I heard, she said, "If you would agree to help me I can get you the money you need." I said "Billy I can't guarantee you anything, but I will work my tail off for you." We agreed, she got me the money I needed to finish getting the center complete and up and running.

Now we are four years behind in all our obligations. Billy lost the election to become Mayor. In 1997 the city elected Charles Smithgall, Mayor.

In 1998 all hell started again in my life. There was another hauler. He was white he also was much larger then I was. He also did campaigning for Mayor Smithgall and in return the Mayor told him they would take my recycling business and give it to him. They were so out spoken about what was going to happen to me and my business until that haulers nephew came to my business and said the Mayor is going to let my uncle have this business. I knew there was some truth in what they were saying. There was another hauler, he was also white. He called me up and said "Willie can I come down there and talk to you." We were supposed to have an Independent Haulers Association and this guy was the vice president, so I welcomed him and said come on down. When he came down we were talking and I was very careful of what I said to him. He asked if he could look around. I said why not this was his first time in the center. As he was looking around I was explaining to him how everything works. I was hoping that he would say let me bring all my recycling to you. Instead he said "let me buy all your equipment." My response was did I hear you right? He said yes. I stopped and said to him I want to make sure you hear me because I am only going to say this one time. You get the hell out of my yard and don't ever come back. Mayor Smithgall was sworn in and tried to find someone who was as racist and devious as he was. He went through two or three sanitation people in his first two years as mayor. He could not find people to work the way he wanted them too, so that delayed his plan.

My younger brother, Winston, who had lived with us for four year had received his diploma and left for the Navy February 8, 1983.

In 1994 my brother Kevin was very sick down in Fort Myers, Florida. I had a friend of mine who was a patient at Hershey Medical Center and asked him to speak to the doctor to have my brother released to his care. The doctor agreed and we moved him and his furniture here. My brother did not have a will so I had taken my attorney to his house in Hershey and we drew up a will. I was made executor of his estate here and in Florida. We were left out of his will. I remember my attorney telling me "you do not have to hand over the house in Florida." I said that is not what he wanted. Kevin Passed in 1994. In 1995 our second son graduated and decided to go to the police academy. My youngest son Terrence graduated 1997 and went to a community college then left for the Marines. In 1998 as Elizabeth and I looked back over the years we could see just how good God had been to us. My father passed in 1999.

The 20th century closed and the millennium year 2000 unfolds. Just as my friend and mentor Jim Hyson said, "Willie they are not going to let you have this business. It is too big for a black man." As I sit here at my desk, I just want to walk you through fifteen years of modern day oppression and slavery. Let me say this it does not matter if they are democrats or republicans, but the people who worked very hard from 1998-2005 to run us out of business were republicans. In 2000 Mayor Smithgall was able to find someone just as racist and deceitful as he was. That's when all hell broke loose again in my life. I remember the new head of sanitation coming to the office and introduced herself to my wife and me. I said to my wife this is trouble. As I stated that the Mayor and the split council wanted a one hauler system and I was the one hauler that stood in their way because many of the other haulers had supported his campaign. He had to be careful how he treated them, so he gave his new sanitation person full reign. Along with her, he requested a lady that lived close by keep watch on us and that's when everything started.

We finally got the business up and running, all construction was complete and things were looking up. We knew we had a rough road ahead but we were persistent and at large we had God on our side and we had each other. We could make it. After this new person learned her way around, she and her boss went after the black haulers. The administration used every Government office at their disposal to run us out of business even to that neighbor. Although it was hard we had two employees and I was the only big truck driver. We could not afford to pay for a cdl driver. We did not have that much work. So I would run the small truck in the day and the big truck in the evening. All though we were working towards getting out of the hauler business and going full time into the recycling business this administration kept us in the hauler business through of their attacks.

The woman the Mayor hired to help him put me out of business would document every move I made from the time I opened the gate till the time I closed the gate. She put everything on paper. She even went so far as to tell them she saw me urinate outside. She recorded seeing me meeting with a friend she stated "I saw Shell and another man walking around inside his fence." She had over 100 documented things that I had supposedly done. She watched me from the time the gate opened at 6:50 am until we closed at 5:10pm.

To show just how unjust the justice system is the city filed charges against me in the low district court. Just to show you how the local District Justice handled this case. Because he knew the woman and he knew me and he was black so he decided not to hear the so called case and kept himself from taken a stand. He sent the case to a white District Justice. The maximum amount the local district justice can fine you is $8,000.00. The city asked the District Justice for ex amount of money for each violation. It totaled $20,000.00. The black District Justice called me up and said "I did you a favor, I told the local District Justice he could not fine you that much, our maximum was $8,000.00.

In 2001 I was introduced to Attorney Allen Taylor, and he began to help me. I had been complaining to him about this lady, he suggested I put up some no trespassing signs. Hoping we could get her in court and that we could come to some kind of agreement. Then she would stop. My attorney was able to prove that she was working for the Mayor. When we got her into court the Mayor showed up on her behalf. He had told the local district justice that she had been assigned to watch my every move and to document it because I was always singing gospel songs. She asked the judge to stop me from singing all those gospel songs, stating that's all he does. The judge and everyone else just looked at her.

Even though they could not stop my singing. I said "I know her pastor and I am going to give him a call." I ask him to come to my office so I can speak to him about one of his members. He said yes. He came down and I let him sit in my chair and I opened up to him hoping that he would act as a go between and find out what my wife and I needed to do in order for her to stop her vicious attacks on us. Well that black Negro preacher took everything I shared with him and used it against me. Her attacks continued until spring of 2002. I was leaving the transfer station when another hauler stopped me and said "well you don't have to worry about your neighbor anymore. I remember I said oh I thought she had gone on vacation or something. When I got back to the office I learned that she was cutting her grass and had a heart attack. Her funeral was held at that black Negro preacher church. That black Negro Democrat city council who that republic Mayor had requested to help destroy me was also present at the funeral, all because they wanted a one hauler system.

At her funeral there was that Mayor. In his remark he stated "we will take care of this." Once again all hell escalated. Now the local police were used. I believe this one police officer had been assigned to harass my drivers. Every time he saw them, he would stop them. The sanitation person would follow them in unmarked cars. The next thing I know I was receiving citations in the mail. Under that administration I received over 100 citations. Your hauler is throwing recycling in the trash. That police officer even stopped my employees for not wearing the green lighted vests and gave them tickets. I remember a preacher friend of mine Rev. T who played the piano for that black Negro preacher for two years. He came to me one day and said "man am I glad to get away from there." For the whole two years I was there your name came across that pulpit every Sunday.

As I stated things were tuning around. Although we only had two trucks, one roll off and one pick up and a trailer behind the pick up to put the recycling in. In January 2001, the county contracted out its facility to outside haulers and they bid out all the equipment. They had everything already in place all I had to do was be the lowest bid and then buy the equipment. I remember it like it was yesterday. We really did not have any money and in order to submit a bid you needed either a bond or ten percent down of the total bid. Well let me just say again repeat Malachi 3:10 "Bring ye all the tithes into the storehouse, that there may be meat in mine house, and prove me now herewith, saith the Lord of hosts, if I will not open you the windows of heaven, and pour you out a blessing, that there shall not be room enough to receive it." Well that night God spoke to me again and told me to put the bid together. I told Elizabeth we are going to win this bid. She responded how are you going to get the money to put down and to get the packer truck? I said I don't know yet. The county is taking bids on all the equipment. We had a small packer truck and the county was selling there's.

After the bid was all together the Lord spoke to me and said go talk to Ray Caulber at the bank. I went and talked to Ray and told him I needed him to do me a favor. He said "Willie, what is it?" I need you to let me have a certified check for $20,000.00. I want to bid on the county contract for trash removal. I remember it as though it was yesterday. Ray looked at me and said" Willie you want me to get fired?" I can't do that. I said

Ray here's how it works, you make the check out to the county, and I am going to bid and take the check with me. If I win the bid they hold it until I get the performance bond. If I don't get the bid they give it back to me right then and there and I'll bring it back to you. All you have to do is void it out. Ray said "Willie you better not cause me to lose my job." I said I won't. Ray gave me the check and I ran up to the county. It was ten o'clock in the morning and the bid opening was at eleven that morning. All bids had to be stamped and dated the clerk said you just made it. I said yes ma'am.

Well they open all the bids. They said the amount of the bid. There were only four bids and we were the last one to be opened. I sat there and listened as they said them and thought I am lower than them. With each bid I knew I was lower than them all. I knew the Lord had opened the window to heaven one more time. I came back to my office and told my wife that day and said baby we got the contract. I then went to the bank and told Ray we won the bid. At first I thanked Ray for believing in me. He did not want to be in a position where he could help but didn't help me. Ok Willie what happens to the check? I said they hold the check until I get the performance bond.

The next day I received a call from the county office reminding me that before they could reward my company this contract I have to have a performance bond and I only had 30 days. No company here would even accept my application so I asked the county office if they knew of any companies that I could call. They gave me the number of two companies. One was here in Lancaster and the other in Philadelphia. The one in Philadelphia assured me of a performance bond. After I received the certificate I took it to the county and they returned the check. I returned the check back to Ray as I had said I would. He said now I can breathe good luck, Willie. I said thank you Ray.

After getting the bond, the county seemed to be very happy with us and very helpful. They even shared with us that the city had come in contact with them saying that they should get a lawyer and get out of that contract because the city was going to put Shell out of business. This was in the year 2001. Thank God the county did not listen to them. In 1 John 4:4 is says, "Ye are of God, little children, and have overcome them because greater is he that is in you, than he that is in the world." We serviced the county from 2001-2009. After I received that contract in June 2001 everything as far as the business was turning around, but the attacks kept coming. The only good thing we had was a steady income to help us fight these attacks.

~From Dark Days to Brighter Days~

"Weeping may endure for a night,
but joy
cometh in the morning."
Psalm 30:5b

As we move into the year 2002, the attacks kept coming but the business was getting better. This section covers the year between 2002 to the present 2015. February 28, these are the years I call from Dark days to Bright Days, disappointing days to hurtful days to modern day slavery.

As I walk through this journey for the next 12 years and two months as the year 2002 unfolds so did my life, it went into another world that I would not wish on anyone. That year 2002, the lady who had been giving us hell had a massive heart attack. We hurt for her family and never expected anything like that would happen. After her death, Mayor Smithgall turned up the attacks. He used every government agency he could convince to help. From law enforcement to D.E.P to Child Labor law. Even worse we received a letter from some government agencies that we had to respond to and the attacks kept on coming until the city landed us in court. The recycle center was shut down for six months. Thanks to Attorney Al Taylor, Councilman Ted Dautch, Mrs. Alice Jackson who was the director of Base and Mr. Derrick Steven and after paying the $30,000.00 plus agreeing to pay $3,000.00 a month and accepting more zoning restrictions they allowed me to reopen.

That did not stop the attacks. This time it was stressful and was beginning to take its toll on my wife Elizabeth. I could see it. So I decided to hire a part time secretary to come in and help her out. The hauler business was picking up and we were on the rise, even with all the attacks. God was blessing us to the point that we needed a bigger truck. Although we needed a bigger truck we did not have the money to buy one but thanks to my brother Johnnie who worked for the sanitation in New York. After explaining my situation to him and our need for a bigger truck, he said brother come over, the sanitation department is having an auction. The next week I went to New York and we went to the auction and I was able to buy a truck. It was a huge step up. After getting the new truck and a partition security, things were looking well. In the mist of it all the attacks kept coming. During this time, however, my life went into another world. November 16, 2002 at 4 pm my wife had a massive heart attack and passed away in my arms. At one point in time I did not want to live. That November

16th through 23rd were the worse days of my life.

As I grieved the loss of not only my wife but the love of my life and best friend, and still trying to hold the business together a New Year, 2003, began to unfold. I was going through hell. The secretary that I hired to work with my wife for the last seven months knew how to run the office just as my wife had. She had gone through a lot with my wife when it came to the business in the office. I also had a friend of the family who knew how much I was hurting. They came in to help out in the office. The only regret was that they could not understand what I was going though and it caused me to act out sometimes under pressure to the point that I would take it out on my secretary. One day with no warning both of them got up and walked out of the office and left me empty handed. But I thank God for His comforting words in Psalm 37:3, 4 "Trust in the Lord, and do good; so shalt thou dwell in the land, and verily thou shalt be fed. Delight thy self also in the Lord; and he shall give thee the desires of thine heart." I want to thank my friend and accountant Pam Bazella. I called her and explained to her what had happened and she said

"Don't worry we'll get someone in the office." The next day I was blessed with another secretary who worked for me for three years before moving to another state. I want to thank my nephew Dorsey Summerall, who stepped up and ran the business for me until I could regain my strength.

I did not know which way to turn, but thanks to my brothers, sisters, friends and mentor Derrick Steven and my neighbor who lived across the street from the business Leroy Thomas I was making it through. My brother Andrew would come over and run loads for me. My brother Roosevelt would call me every day just to make sure I was alright. My brother Nathaniel would come over and stay two and three days at a time and my brother Johnnie would call every morning and night. My brother Winston would call daily as well as my older sister Arbra and say bro I have my whole church praying for you. My sister Belinda would also call to make sure I was eating right. She would tell me what to buy at the store. I also want to thank my friend Leroy who made sure that I had food. He would cook and bring me a plate across the street at least three to four days per week. I also want to thank my Brother Willie and Francine Morant who own the restaurant behind the recycling center. They would allow me to come there and eat for free. I thank my friend Dr. White who counselled me many times and assisted me financially. I would also like to thank my friend and Mentor Derrick Steven who had a coffee shop and came on board after my friend and mentor Jim Hyson had passed. Derrick would come whenever I needed him. Even then the attacks from the city kept coming.

As the New Year 2004 unfolds former Mayor Smithgall and the new sanitation person along with that black Negro preacher and the black Negro councilman kept supporting the administration in their attacks not only on me but on all black haulers to the point that some haulers were afraid to go out. Every time you look around they were sending you citations in the mail. There were four local District Justice offices in the city and they would send you one from each one of the offices. They even used the child labor law department. I remember I had a friend of mine whose son had been suspended from school and she needed someone to look after him and my secretary asked if he could hang out at the office for three days, and I agreed. The last day the boy asked me if he could go with me on the truck. I let him ride along. The next thing I knew I was sent information from the child labor law department saying I was hiring under age children. They even had pictures of the boy on the truck. I thank my friend Derrick who helped me get through that one also.

One day I was working, up came this black Negro councilman and he had one bag of recycling in his hand and as he walked closer to me I could see the Mayor and another person in a car. He looked towards the car as he was saying I'm here. The Lord spoke to me and told me something I already knew this black Negro was working with the Mayor to destroy me and my business. Since that day he had not come back to the recycling center, since the summer of 2004 till the present 2015.

Well as 2004 came to a close, my wife had been gone for two years now. I had not had a phone call or visit from not even one of my sons. I remember sitting at my friend's restaurant one Saturday and telling him how my three sons were ignoring me since their mother had passed, to the point I felt like they were blaming me for her death. In the past twelve years and four months since my wife's passing, we have had thanksgiving dinner twice together. I have received two birthday cards and have had maybe twenty to thirty visitors to the house they grew up in. I have had maybe ten visitors to the business that their mother and I started. It seems to me when their mother passed the family passed also. I wish I had more things to say about my three sons but at the present time, it is what it is.

As the year 2005 began to unfold it was an election year. The former Mayor Smithgall backed off somewhat, the new candidate for Mayor was a Democrat. I had been through so much with former Mayor Smithgall and administration. I remember talking to the Lord and saying I can't take another four years of this. During 2005 I had been stopped on Duke Street by a police officer who was also a city inspector for big trucks. I was in the restaurant and my truck was parked. When I came out this officer was inspecting my truck. He took my truck out of service because the tire treads were a little low. I tried to explain to him that they were on order and the next day I had an appointment to have new ones put on the truck. He said you can't move this truck. I asked him will he let me take it to my business. He replied no. I said I am only asking to go eight blocks. He said no. I knew this was an attack. After he left I decided to take the truck back to my lot that I was renting. That officer made up his mind that he would charge me. He went to look for my truck the next day. The garage came to my lot and put the new tires on. The officers found were I was. He then sited me for moving the truck. I went to see my friend and attorney Al Taylor who was in the same building as another attorney who told us to go see this lawyer and he could probably make this all go away. He is well known, so Al and I went to see him and explained everything to him. He said he did not know anything about me but he had read about me. He took the case, at that time I did not know he was running for Mayor. After I learned that he had been selected by the Democrat to run in the city for Mayor I went to him and had a conversation with him about what his position was on the trash system. He responded by saying I do not want to put anyone out of business, I just want to make sure everyone has a hauler. I took him at his word, especially since he was my attorney also. I came back and shared that with the other haulers and we all supported him. Well, after the election in November 2005 was over you had a full slate Democrats and a democratic Mayor who was supposed to help the working class, especially minorities. Well, 2005 came to an end and in 2006 a new Mayor, new council, and new rules came into play.

The first thing on the new administrations agenda was to get a one hauler system in place. That went on for the first six months. It did not matter what the citizens had to say, even when they showed up at council meetings. With a full house the Mayor and council did not respect the wishes of the people at any time. People were saying they were not paying the new trash bills and were being told if they did not pay the bills they would be turned over to the collections bureau. Many of the haulers had contracts with the citizens of the city. This happens in the fall of 2006, October of that same year this new Mayor and city council had their way. I was the only hauler that had a lifetime contract with the residents, which read that it could only be cancelled by me and the residents that signed the contract. This Mayor and the council ran an article in the paper saying that the city will not honor self-renewing contracts that year.

As the year 2006 came to an end and the 2007 unfolded, the city had taken 900 to 1,000 customers. At the same time they had fired the person that was head of the sanitation department under the former Mayor. They hired a woman that would do all their dirty work for them. She didn't last long, they hired a gentleman that would do some of their dirty work and knew his way around. He had contacts with the D.E.P and they got them to try and destroy me. This person from the D.E.P would follow me around town like he was a police officer. They used him to go to some of my customers and had them cancel their contracts with me. The customer would call me up and tell me they had no problem with me and they liked the way I did business but they did not want to deal with the D.E.P. Therefore I am going to have to cancel my contract with you.

When I say modern day slavery here is an

example, I had been doing business with the L.C.S.W.M.A for over 30 years at that time, when I was running five minutes late I would call them and ask them to keep the gate open, they had no problem with that. When the letter came from the D.E.P saying that the new rule stated that a trash truck cannot hold trash in it for more than four hours in a resident area where I normally parked my truck. I knew it would be within the four mile journey and knew that the D.E.P person knew where I kept my truck. So that day I had taken it down to a friend of mine, they found my truck down there and they threatened him. The next day he told me he had a visitor from the board of health saying they know I have a trash truck parked in my lot. Willie I don't need these people bothering me, I said I understand. Well that went on through the year 2007 we were losing customers, being followed by the D.E.P, being cited and fined by the D.E.P. also being followed by the new sanitation chief.

Now as 2008 beings to unfold things were not getting any better. We had fell behind on bills and the city used that to get us back in the local court that they control and used to their advantage. They tried to use the court to their advantage and closed me down for non-payment, which was the main reason, but thank be to God, and the many companies I was dealing with, and my Attorney Al Taylor. After talking together with the Mayor I had to come up with $25,000.00 in order to reopen. I got on the phone and called a company that I did business with and told them my situation, they responded "Willie I can have you a check in the morning by nine o'clock. I said ok and thanked them and letting them know either I or my Attorney would pick up the check. The next morning Al and I went and got the check. By ten o'clock that morning we had what the Mayor had requested. He would not accept a company check. He wanted a bank certified check. My friend Ray Caulber had retired from the bank I had been doing business with for over fifteen years. I had taken the check to them and asked if they would issue me a certified check. They said no. I said ok thank you. I had just opened a pension checking account at another bank and had got to know the manager. I went in to see her and explained my situation to her. She said is this check any good and I said yes it was. She called the bank the check was drawn on and got verification that the check was good. Everything checked out good and she issued me a bank certified check in the amount of $25,000.00. I told her she would always have a friend in me. Thank you Pastor Yvette Withfield. Well, we were allowed to reopen.

Reopening, and staying alive with losing 1,000 customers, the market dropping and fuel prices increasing. Things were not getting any better. People were calling me and coming into the office and saying "I don't want to leave you. You have been picking up my trash since you been in business, but I don't want my credit ruined. The city said if I don't pay this bill they will put me in the credit bureau."

Well that same year after the city had used its governmental power and its attacks to force the residents to pay them, it caused us to not be able to continue paying our bills. The city was the main one at $3,000.00 per month. So that year we had filed a law suit against the city for interfering with our contracts. The first judge ruled in our favor in 2009. He sent the case to his immediate judge who kept it in her hands for fifteen months. My attorney and I would meet there for five minutes and the attorney for the city would say" we have nothing to offer you as far as this case goes." This went on until the next election.

During that same year they were still looking for a way to destroy my business. They used the government again and any outside business's they could use for example the Child Labor Board, D.E.P Ect... As I stated earlier we won the bid to service the county contract. In 2001 and every time it was up for bid, we would win because we were an independent company and we were very close to all the facilities which gave us some advantage until 2009. When I and three other haulers put in our bids, I was $100,000.00 under them. A larger hauler from the State of Pennsylvania to my knowledge came in $73,000.00 under my bid. I could not prove it but I just knew something was fishy with that so did my attorney.

Another New Year was approaching, 2009 came to a close and 2010 came in, along with the election year. The Recycling Center was rebounding, but that was not enough to keep the company running and to meet all our responsibilities. I knew that the city was making their way back to the local court where they had control. I was forced to file bankruptcy not only for the business but also personal. The bankruptcy in 2010 put them at bay for a while.

When 2011 came in we went back to the negotiation table. January 2011 the city put an offer on the table, they offered to pay my attorney, forgive my debt I owed them and for me to turn over all my residential customers then within six months. I was to turn over all customers, basically I was to leave town. At that meeting the mediator judge, the mayor, the city attorney and my attorney who was from Philadelphia had been negotiating with out my knowledge until that night January 14 at when I learned my attorney had sold me out. They had been negotiating without me. My attorney came to the meeting with how many hours and how much the city would have to pay him. I had another attorney Allen Taylor and my nephew there with me. I stopped the meeting and asked the mediation judge if we could take a break. We went out of the court room and I listened as Allan and my nephew talked. They both agreed that there was nothing in the settlement agreement in my favor. I never said a word, I just listened. Before we went back in I said let's have we word of prayer. The Lord said don't accept this. I told my attorney that I am not accepting this agreement. I told the judge this was not acceptable and she then asked what would be acceptable to you. I also informed the judge that I had an order saying that the city is not to interfere with my customers until the end of 2011. The judge asked my attorney if he had a copy of the order. He said no, but I knew that he did. He had struck a deal with the city. The judge request a copy of the order be sent to her. The mediator judge also wants me to put something in writing that she could take to the city.

The next day I called my friend and attorney Beverly Britton Fraser and explained to her what had happened. My friend Beverly put together a letter and faxed it over to me and said give this to her. I faxed over that letter and another letter over to my attorney in Philadelphia for him to give it to the mediator judge. He sat on it.

They were trying to force me into signing the settlement agreement, I refused and my attorney in Philadelphia stopped representing me. I had to find another attorney within one week, because of the bankruptcy that put everything on hold. I hired another attorney out of Philadelphia who basically worked in mediation. In February, I received a so called settlement agreement by mail and it said you have fourteen days to sign it. If you do not sign it the court will sign it for you. I called the Philadelphia attorney and he said that there was nothing he could do. I had a friend in Harrisburg, Reggie, I called him and he put me in touch with a lawyer in D.C. He in turn put me in touch with Attorney Foley who was not a civil suit lawyer, but a negotiation attorney. He knew how to keep this at bay. At the same time, I had filed chapter 11 and chapter 13 bankruptcies, business and personal.

In March that same year we met with the negotiation judge, again that attorney who had sold me out at the last meeting was at this one. At this meeting it was the city attorney, my brothers Johnnie and Winston and my former attorney who I had already fired. The mediator judge would not remove him from the case. He asked her to allow him to remain on the case. She honored his request. When this meeting was over one more meeting was scheduled to take place in the summer.

The mediation judge called another meeting that was in April or May that same year in her chamber. At that meeting there was that attorney and two of my brothers Johnnie and Winston. At that meeting she stressed that I give her something in writing that she could take to the city. Thanks to my friend Derrick we put another proposal together and sent it to her and the city. We sent her a letter and told her that if she tried to make the city give Shell one dime we would appeal it. Well she backed up and the case just sat there. Now no actions were being taken as this was happening we were still proceeding through bankruptcy court.

At this meeting it was just the mediator, the attorney, I had fired, and my brothers. We met her in her chamber, I remember she kept saying give me one thing I can take to the city. I said I've already given you something. She said Mr. Shell, "I can be your worst enemy." I said "why, because I won't go along with you and this attorney who should not be at this table." You have my offer send the case back to the previous judge. She said "no this is my case and I am keeping it." Well, that meeting was over and that was in the summer 2011.

One Friday I went over to my friend Willie's Restaurant, which is just behind my business. There was my friend Paul Caulber having dinner with an attorney from Erie, Pa. Paul introduced me to this attorney whose name was Caleb Nichols. Paul had been telling him about my business, how the city had been attacking me and how they just took the hauler business from me. He had also told him that I was the only on who would stand up and fight them and that I had filed a law suit against them. That same day Attorney Caleb said "I would like to take a look at the file and who filed it for you." So I told him the name of the attorney who had filed it. I also told him the name of the attorney I fired. He responded "Oh, I know him. He and I went to law school together but that was about forty years ago. I will still help you if I can." That same day Caleb Nichols came on board as my attorney. That was June 8, 2011.

The only good thing about this was that the bankruptcy court put a stay on everything. But the city never stopped even at the bankruptcy hearing. It used all its power to try to get the bankruptcy judge to either turn my business to chapter 7 or dismiss it, but thanks to my attorney Lawrence from Harrisburg, my attorney Foley from Philadelphia, the trustee and the bankruptcy judge they were not able to manipulate the proceedings. The city solicitor, who I talked about earlier that would show up at my business anytime he felt like it was the only witness for the city. He had taken over one hundred pictures. He even stated to the court that he had taken all these pictures himself. As we left the court room both of my attorney's said you can sue that guy. Well they were not able to use this judge like they did the other judge. She kept the stay order in place, which kept them at bay until July 2012 when we were able to get the conformation plan approved.

Even after the plan had been confirmed, the attacks did not stop. The city then went back to the bankruptcy court and asked them to allow them to enforce zoning ordinance. As the year 2012 came to a close and 2013 the New Year unfolded, the attacks kept coming. The bankruptcy court gave them permission, which was all they needed. There they used the local, state, and county to get a temporary injunction against me. The temporary injunction was in place until June 2013 and the attacks kept coming. We filed a motion to the bankruptcy court to stay the local court order. The bankruptcy court would not stay the local order. September 2014 ended the temporary injunction. This injunction caused the business to drop to twenty five percent of operation, which meant we had to reduce costs and lay off employees and cut overhead just to stay afloat. This continued into 2014.

In 2014 the harassment continued to mount, the city had taken us back to the local court, now asking the local court for a permanent injunction. Again the local court granted them the request that meant that now they have the right to lock the gate to my business. Even that was not enough. They requested the IRS to levy my bank accounts and the accounts of the companies I did business with. Not only did the IRS levy a company that

I did business with but they even levied resident trash customers. I knew that the only way they could have got the information of my customers was from the city. On January 15, 2015 attorney Jerry Finefrock and I had a meeting with the IRS person, I asked him how did he get my customers information, he said he subpoenaed the city. I knew that the city had to put names to the addresses. The city started requesting that the haulers send a customer list. I never sent one name to the city, only addresses. They used the Lancaster County tax office attorney to help in their attacks in September 2014.

Because of their many attacks and the loss of business I was forced to file personal bankruptcy for property tax. Thanks to attorney Alaine Grbach, even though the attorney for the county tax office tried very hard to get the case dismissed, the bankruptcy court stayed our request. The attacks did not stop; they kept coming even after I filed my personal bankruptcy in September 2014, the city recruited the Lancaster County Solid Waste Authority that I had been doing business with since 1974. They sent me a letter in September 2014 saying because of your bankruptcy and your credit we are putting you on a cash only payment. So that meant every time you pull upon the scale you must have cash, no credit cards, and no checks cash only. After I received that letter I wrote to the Lancaster County Solid Waste Authority, Directors and the County Commissioners. I did receive a phone call from the Lancaster Solid Waste Authority director; after a long conversation he stated if you don't like our decision then sue us. My response to him" I never thought I would hear such words come from someone in the position you're in".

While working through the bankruptcy court we were also working with the U.S District court to resolve the mediation case. Caleb Nichols came on board in June and took over the mediation case and so called settlement agreement. There were seven conference calls between the mediation judge, my attorney and myself. Each time there was a conversation the judge would say you will have my decision by next month. The next month would come and go, still no decision. Attorney Caleb Nichols wrote a letter to the district court, and the mediation judge's boss asking him to make the mediation judge render her opinion on the case. Instead of rendering her opinion, she rendered a decision that meant that I had agreed to the so called mutual release and settlement agreement. That decision came down on December 30, 2011. On January 5, 2012 attorney Caleb L Nichols filed a memorandum opinion to the district court to ask the judge to overturn the mediation decision. He refused. In June of 2012, we hired an attorney Clifford Reider. Attorney Caleb L Nichols and attorney Clifford Reider filed to the third circuit asking the third circuit to overturn the district court's decision. They upheld the decision.

Just recently, God saw fit to send Attorney Richard Puleo into my life. At the present time both Richard and I have had several conversations. He has not and he said will never ask for a dime to represent me. We run into one another at the gym and he said, "I don't know why God bought us together but I am going to enter my appearance as a co-council on your behalf." This was Wednesday March 04, 2015. He has vowed to get me out of all these legal binds that I have entangled in for over

20 years for no good reason. I can only state what David said in Psalm 30:5 "For his anger endureth, but a moment; in his favour is life: weeping may endure for a night but joy cometh in the morning." Job 13:15 says, "Though he slays me yet will I trust in him." In Malachi 3:10 again it says, "Prove me now herewith, saith the Lord of hosts, if I will not open you the windows of heaven, and pour you out a blessing, that there shall not be room enough to receive it." I believe the word of God. He has kept me through all of these trails.

As I close this book or volume 1 of my story, on this historical day, March 8, 2015, which marks the fiftieth anniversary of Bloody Sunday and as President Obama speaks about injustice that not only in Ferguson but all over the nation, the gates of my business have been locked by the city. I have been locked out of my own business because I have taken a stand for my rights. Nevertheless, after all I have been through I'M STILL STANDING.

…And I'm Still Standing is available on Amazon.com

21656225R00059

Made in the USA
Middletown, DE
07 July 2015